Suffrage Songs and Verses

Suffrage Songs and Verses

Charlotte Perkins Gilman

MINT EDITIONS

Suffrage Songs and Verses was first published in 1911.

This edition published by Mint Editions 2021.

ISBN 9781513269856 | E-ISBN 9781513274850

Published by Mint Editions®

MINT EDITIONS

minteditionbooks.com

Publishing Director: Jennifer Newens
Design & Production: Rachel Lopez Metzger
Typesetting: Westchester Publishing Services

Contents

She Walketh Veiled and Sleeping

She walketh veiled and sleeping,
For she knoweth not her power;
She obeyeth but the pleading
Of her heart, and the high leading
Of her soul, unto this hour.
Slow advancing, halting, creeping,
Comes the Woman to the hour!—
She walketh veiled and sleeping,
For she knoweth not her power.

Coming

Because the time is ripe, the age is ready,
Because the world her woman's help demands,
Out of the long subjection and seclusion
Come to our field of warfare and confusion
The mother's heart and hands.

Long has she stood aside, endured and waited,
While man swung forward, toiling on alone;
Now, for the weary man, so long ill-mated,
Now, for the world for which she was created,
Comes woman to her own.

Not for herself! though sweet the air of freedom;
Not for herself, though dear the new-born power;
But for the child, who needs a nobler mother,
For the whole people, needing one another,
Comes woman to her hour.

LOCKED INSIDE

She beats upon her bolted door,
    With faint weak hands;
Drearily walks the narrow floor;
Sullenly sits, blank walls before;
    Despairing stands.

Life calls her, Duty, Pleasure, Gain—
    Her dreams respond;
But the blank daylights wax and wane,
Dull peace, sharp agony, slow pain—
    No hope beyond.

Till she comes a thought! She lifts her head,
    The world grows wide!
A voice—as if clear words were said—
"Your door, O long imprisonéd,
    Is locked inside!"

Now

With God Above—Beneath—Beside—
    Without—Within—and Everywhere;
Rising with the resistless tide
    Of life, and Sure of Getting There.

Patient with Nature's long delay,
    Proud of our conscious upward swing;
Not sorry for a single day,
    And Not Afraid of Anything!

With Motherhood at last awake—
    With Power to Do and Light to See—
Women may now begin to Make
    The People we are Meant to Be!

WOMEN OF TO-DAY

You women of today who fear so much
The women of the future, showing how
The dangers of her course are such and such—
                What are you now?

Mothers and Wives and Housekeepers, forsooth!
Great names, you cry, full scope to rule and please,
Room for wise age and energetic youth!—
                But are you these?

Housekeepers? Do you then, like those of yore,
Keep house with power and pride, with grace and ease?
No, you keep servants only! What is more—
                You don't keep these!

Wives, say you? Wives! Blessed indeed are they
Who hold of love the everlasting keys,
Keeping their husbands' hearts! Alas the day!
                You don't keep these!

And mothers? Pitying Heaven! Mark the cry
From cradle death-beds! Mothers on their knees!
Why, half the children born, as children, die!
                You don't keep these!

And still the wailing babies come and go,
And homes are waste, and husbands' hearts fly far;
There is no hope until you dare to know
                The thing you are!

Boys Will Be Boys

"Boys will be boys," and boys have had their day;
  Boy-mischief and boy-carelessness and noise
Extenuated all, allowed, excused and smoothed away,
    Each duty missed, each damaging wild act,
    By this meek statement of unquestioned fact—
        Boys will be boys!

Now, "women will be women." Mark the change;
  Calm motherhood in place of boisterous youth;
No warfare now; to manage and arrange,
    To nurture with wise care, is woman's way,
    In peace and fruitful industry her sway,
        In love and truth.

For Fear

For fear of prowling beasts at night
    They blocked the cave;
Women and children hid from sight,
    Men scarce more brave.

For fear of warrior's sword and spear
    They barred the gate;
Women and children lived in fear,
    Men lived in hate.

For fear of criminals today
    We lock the door;
Women and children still to stay
    Hid evermore.

Come out! Ye need no longer hide!
    What fear you now?
No wolf nor lion waits outside—
    Only a cow.

Come out! The world approaches peace,
    War nears its end;
No warrior watches your release—
    Only a friend.

Come out! The night of crime has fled—
    Day is begun;
Here is no criminal to dread—
    Only your son.

The world, half yours, demands your care,
    Waken and come!
Make it a woman's world; safe, fair,
    Garden and home.

Mother to Child

How best can I serve thee, my child! My child!
Flesh of my flesh and dear heart of my heart!
Once thou wast within me—I held thee—I fed thee—
By the force of my loving and longing I led thee—
        Now we are apart!

I may blind thee with kisses and crush with embracing,
Thy warm mouth in my neck and our arms interlacing;
But here in my body my soul lives alone,
And thou answerest me from a house of thine own—
        That house which I builded!

Which we builded together, thy father and I;
In which thou must live, O my darling, and die!
Not one stone can I alter, one atom relay—
Not to save or defend thee or help thee to stay—
        That gift is completed!

How best can I serve thee? O child, if they knew
How my heart aches with loving! How deep and how true,
How brave and enduring, how patient, how strong,
How longing for good and how fearful of wrong,
        Is the love of thy mother!

Could I crown thee with riches! Surround, overflow thee
With fame and with power till the whole world should know thee;
With wisdom and genius to hold the world still,
To bring laughter and tears, joy and pain, at thy will,
        Still—*thou* mightst not be happy!

Such have lived—and in sorrow. The greater the mind
The wider and deeper the grief it can find.
The richer, the gladder, the more thou canst feel
The keen stings that a lifetime is sure to reveal.
        O my child! Must thou suffer?

Is there no way my life can save thine from a pain?
Is the love of a mother no possible gain?
No labor of Hercules—search for the Grail—
No way for this wonderful love to avail?
              God in Heaven—O teach me!

My prayer has been answered. The pain thou must bear
Is the pain of the world's life which thy life must share.
Thou art one with the world—though I love thee the best;
And to save thee from pain I must save all the rest—
              Well—with God's help I'll do it.

Thou art one with the rest. I must love thee in them.
Thou wilt sin with the rest; and thy mother must stem
The world's sin. Thou wilt weep, and thy mother must dry
The tears of the world lest her darling should cry.
              I will do it—God helping!

And I stand not alone. I will gather a band
Of all loving mothers from land unto land.
Our children are part of the world! Do ye hear?
They are one with the world—we must hold them all dear!
              Love all for the child's sake!

For the sake of my child I must hasten to save
All the children on earth from the jail and the grave.
For so, and so only, I lighten the share
Of the pain of the world that my darling must bear—
              Even so, and so only!

A QUESTION

Why is it, God, that mother's hearts are made
　　So very deep and wide?
How does it help the world that we should hold
Such welling floods of pain till we are old,
Because when we were young one grave was laid—
One baby died?

THE HOUSEWIFE

Here is the House to hold me—cradle of all the race;
Here is my lord and my love, here are my children dear—
Here is the House enclosing, the dear-loved dwelling place;
Why should I ever weary for aught that I find not here?

Here for the hours of the day and the hours of the night;
Bound with the bands of Duty, rivetted tight;
Duty older than Adam—Duty that saw
Acceptance utter and hopeless in the eyes of the serving squaw.

Food and the serving of food—that is my daylong care;
What and when we shall eat, what and how we shall wear;
Soiling and cleaning of things—that is my task in the main—
Soil them and clean them and soil them—soil them and clean
    them again.

To work at my trade by the dozen and never a trade to know;
To plan like a Chinese puzzle—fitting and changing so;
To think of a thousand details, each in a thousand ways;
For my own immediate people and a possible love and praise.

My mind is trodden in circles, tiresome, narrow and hard,
Useful, commonplace, private—simply a small backyard;
And I the Mother of Nations!—Blind their struggle and vain!—
I cover the earth with my children—each with a housewife's brain.

WEDDED BLISS

"O come and be my mate!" said the Eagle to the Hen;

> "I love to soar, but then
> I want my mate to rest
> Forever in the nest!"
> Said the Hen, "I cannot fly,
> I have no wish to try,

But I joy to see my mate careening through the sky!"
They wed, and cried, "Ah, this is Love, my own!"
And the Hen sat, the Eagle soared, alone.

"O come and be my mate!" said the Lion to the Sheep;

> "My love for you is deep!
> I slay, a Lion should,
> But you are mild and good!"
> Said the sheep, "I do no ill—
> Could not, had I the will—.

But I joy to see my mate pursue, devour and kill."
They wed, and cried, "Ah, this is Love, my own!"
And the Sheep browsed, the Lion prowled, alone.

"O come and be my mate!" said the Salmon to the Clam;

> "You are not wise, but I am.
> I know sea and stream as well,
> You know nothing but your shell."
> Said the Clam, "I'm slow of motion,
> But my love is all devotion,

And I joy to have my mate traverse lake and stream and ocean!"
They wed, and cried, "Ah, this is Love, my own!"
And the Clam sucked, the Salmon swam, alone.

CHARLOTTE PERKINS GILMAN

FEMALES

The female fox she is a fox;
The female whale a whale;
The female eagle holds her place
As representative of race
As truly as the male.

The mother hen doth scratch for her chicks,
And scratch for herself beside;
The mother cow doth nurse her calf,
Yet fares as well as her other half
In the pasture free and wide.

The female bird doth soar in air;
The female fish doth swim;
The fleet-foot mare upon the course
Doth hold her own with the flying horse—
Yea and she beateth him!

One female in the world we find
Telling a different tale.
It is the female of our race,
Who holds a parasitic place
Dependent on the male.

Not so, saith she, ye slander me!
No parasite am I.
I earn my living as a wife;
My children take my very life;
Why should I share in human strife,
To plant and build and buy?

The human race holds highest place
In all the world so wide,
Yet these inferior females wive,
And raise their little ones alive,
And feed themselves beside.

The race is higher than the sex,
Though sex be fair and good;
A Human Creature is your state,
And to be human is more great
Than even womanhood!

The female fox she is a fox;
The female whale a whale;
The female eagle holds her place
As representative of race
As truly as the male.

We As Women

There's a cry in the air about us—
We hear it before, behind—
Of the way in which "We, as women,"
Are going to lift mankind!

With our white frocks starched and ruffled,
And our soft hair brushed and curled—
Hats off! for "We, as women,"
Are coming to save the world.

Fair sisters, listen one moment—
And perhaps you'll pause for ten:
The business of women as women
Is only with men as men!

What we do, "We, as women,"
We have done all through our life;
The work that is ours as women
Is the work of mother and wife.

But to elevate public opinion,
And to lift up erring man,
Is the work of the Human Being;
Let us do it—if we can.

But wait, warm-hearted sisters—
Not quite so fast, so far.
Tell me how we are going to lift a thing
Any higher than we are!

We are going to "purify politics,"
And to "elevate the press."
We enter the foul paths of the world
To sweeten and cleanse and bless.

To hear the high things we are going to do,
And the horrors of man we tell,
One would think, "We, as women," were angels,
And our brothers were fiends of hell.

We, that were born of one mother,
And reared in the self-same place,
In the school and the church together,
We of one blood, one race!

Now then, all forward together!
But remember, every one,
That 'tis not by feminine innocence
The work of the world is done.

The world needs strength and courage,
And wisdom to help and feed—
When, "We, as women" bring these to man,
We shall lift the world indeed.

Girls of To-day

Girls of today! Give ear!
Never since time began
Has come to the race of man
A year, a day, an hour,
So full of promise and power
As the time that now is here!

Never in all the lands
Was there a power so great,
To move the wheels of state,
To lift up body and mind,
To waken the deaf and blind,
As the power that is in your hands!

Here at the gates of gold
You stand in the pride of youth,
Strong in courage and truth,
Stirred by a force kept back
Through centuries long and black,
Armed with a power threefold!

First: You are makers of men!
Then Be the things you preach!
Let your own greatness teach!
When Mothers like this you see
Men will be strong and free—
Then, and not till then!

Second: Since Adam fell,
Have you not heard it said
That men by women are led?
True is the saying—true!
See to it what you do!
See that you lead them well.

Third: You have work of your own!
Maid and mother and wife,

Look in the face of life!
There are duties you owe the race!
Outside your dwelling-place
There is work for you alone!

Maid and mother and wife,
See your own work be done!
Be worthy a noble son!
Help man in the upward way!
Truly, a girl today
Is the strongest thing in life!

WOMEN TO MEN

Dear father, from my cradle I acknowledge
All your wise kindness, tender care, and love,
Through days of kindergarten, school and college.
Now there is one gift lacking—one above
All other gifts of God, this highest trust is,
The one great gift, beyond all power and pelf—
Give me my freedom, father; give me justice,
That I may guard my children and myself.

My brother, you and I were reared together;
We played together, even-handed quite;
We went to school in every kind of weather,
Studied and ranked together as was right.
We work together now and earn our living,
You know how equal is the work we do;
Come, brother, with the love you're always giving,
Give justice! It's for me as well as you.

And you, my lover, kneeling here before me
With tender eyes that burn, warm lips that plead,
Protesting that you worship, aye, adore me;
Begging my love as life's supremest meed,
Vowing to make me happy. Ah, how dare you!
Freedom and happiness have both one key!
Lover and husband, by the love I bear you,
Give justice! I can love you better, free!

Son my own son! Man-child that once was lying
All rosy, tender, helpless on my breast,
Your strength all dimples, your stern voice but crying,
Looking to me for comfort, food and rest,
Asking your life of me, and not another—
And asking not in vain till life be done—
Oh, my boy-baby! Is it I, your mother,
Who comes to ask of justice from her son?

Now to the voter—tax-payer (or shirker),
Please lay your private feelings on the shelf;
O Man-at-large! Friend! Comrade! Fellow-worker;
I am a human being like yourself.
I'm not your wife and mother. Can't be, whether
I would or not: each to his own apart;
But in the world we're people altogether—
Suffrage is not a question of the heart.

Son—Father—Brother—Lover unsupplanted—
We'll talk at home. This thing concerns the nation;
A point of justice which is to be granted
By men to women who are no relation.
Perceive this fact, as salient as a steeple,
Please try to argue from it if you can;
Women have standing-room on earth as people
Outside of their relation to some man.

As wife and sweetheart, daughter, sister, mother,
Each woman privately her views explains;
As people of America—no other—
We claim the right our government maintains.
You who deny it stand in history's pages
Withholding justice! Pitiless and plain
Your record stands down all the brightening ages—
You fought with progress, but you fought in vain.

CHARLOTTE PERKINS GILMAN

Reassurance

Can you imagine nothing better, brother,
Than that which you have always had before?
Have you been so content with "wife and mother,"
      You dare hope nothing more?

Have you forever prized her, praised her, sung her,
The happy queen of a most happy reign?
Never dishonored her, despised her, flung her
      Derision and disdain?

Go ask the literature of all the ages!
Books that were written before women read!
Pagan and Christian, satirists and sages—
      Read what the world has said.

There was no power on earth to bid you slacken
The generous hand that painted her disgrace!
There was no shame on earth too black to blacken
      That much-praised woman-face.

Eve and Pandora!—always you begin it—
The ancients called her Sin and Shame and Death.
"There is no evil without woman in it,"
      The modern proverb saith.

She has been yours in uttermost possession—
Your slave, your mother, your well-chosen bride—
And you have owned in million-fold confession,
      You were not satisfied.

Peace then! Fear not the coming woman, brother.
Owning herself, she giveth all the more.
She shall be better woman, wife and mother
      Than man hath known before.

The Socialist and the Suffragist

Said the Socialist to the Suffragist:
  "My cause is greater than yours!
    You only work for a Special Class,
    We for the gain of the General Mass,
  Which every good ensures!"

Said the Suffragist to the Socialist:
  "You underrate my Cause!
    While women remain a Subject Class,
    You never can move the General Mass,
  With your Economic Laws!"

Said the Socialist to the Suffragist:
  "You misinterpret facts!
    There is no room for doubt or schism
    In Economic Determinism—
  It governs all our acts!"

Said the Suffragist to the Socialist:
  "You men will always find
    That this old world will never move
    More swiftly in its ancient groove
  While women stay behind!"

"A lifted world lifts women up,"
  The Socialist explained.
    "You cannot lift the world at all
    While half of it is kept so small,"
  The Suffragist maintained.

The world awoke, and tartly spoke:
  "Your work is all the same:
    Work together or work apart,
    Work, each of you, with all your heart—
  Just get into the game!"

The Malingerer

Exempt! She "does not have to work!"
     So might one talk
Defending long, bedridden ease,
Weak yielding ankles, flaccid knees,
     With, "I don't have to walk!"

Not have to work. Why not? Who gave
     Free pass to you?
You're housed and fed and taught and dressed
By age-long labor of the rest—
     Work other people do!

What do you give in honest pay
     For clothes and food?—
Then as a shield, defence, excuse,
She offers her exclusive use—
     Her function—Motherhood!

Is motherhood a trade you make
     A living by?
And does the wealth you so may use,
Squander, accumulate, abuse,
     Show motherhood as high?

Or does the motherhood of those
     Whose toil endures,
The farmers' and mechanics' wives,
Hard working servants all their lives—
     Deserve less price than yours?

We're not exempt! Man's world runs on,
     Motherless, wild;
Our servitude and long duress,
Our shameless, harem idleness,
     Both fail to serve the child.

The Anti-Suffragists

Fashionable women in luxurious homes,
With men to feed them, clothe them, pay their bills,
Bow, doff the hat, and fetch the handkerchief;
Hostess or guest; and always so supplied
With graceful deference and courtesy;
Surrounded by their horses, servants, dogs—
These tell us they have all the rights they want.

Successful women who have won their way
Alone, with strength of their unaided arm,
Or helped by friends, or softly climbing up
By the sweet aid of "woman's influence";
Successful any way, and caring naught
For any other woman's unsuccess—
These tell us they have all the rights they want.

Religious women of the feebler sort—
Not the religion of a righteous world,
A free, enlightened, upward-reaching world,
But the religion that considers life
As something to back out of!—whose ideal
Is to renounce, submit, and sacrifice,
Counting on being patted on the head
And given a high chair when they get to heaven—
These tell us they have all the rights they want.

Ignorant women—college bred sometimes,
But ignorant of life's realities
And principles of righteous government,
And how the privileges they enjoy
Were won with blood and tears by those before—
Those they condemn, whose ways they now oppose;
Saying, "Why not let well enough alone?
Our world is very pleasant as it is"—
These tell us they have all the rights they want.

CHARLOTTE PERKINS GILMAN

And selfish women—pigs in petticoats—
Rich, poor, wise, unwise, top or bottom round,
But all sublimely innocent of thought,
And guiltless of ambition, save the one
Deep, voiceless aspiration—to be fed!
These have no use for rights or duties more.
Duties today are more than they can meet,
And law insures their right to clothes and food—
These tell us they have all the rights they want.

And, more's the pity, some good women, too;
Good, conscientious women with ideas;
Who think—or think they think—that woman's cause
Is best advanced by letting it alone;
That she somehow is not a human thing,
And not to be helped on by human means,
Just added to humanity—an "L"—
A wing, a branch, an extra, not mankind—
These tell us they have all the rights they want.

And out of these has come a monstrous thing,
A strange, down-sucking whirlpool of disgrace,
Women uniting against womanhood,
And using that great name to hide their sin!
Vain are their words as that old king's command
Who set his will against the rising tide.
But who shall measure the historic shame
Of these poor traitors—traitors are they all—
To great Democracy and Womanhood!

The Anti and the Fly

The fly upon the Cartwheel
    Thought he made all the Sound;
He thought he made the Cart go on—
    And made the wheels go round.

The Fly upon the Cartwheel
    Has won undying fame
For Conceit that was colossal,
    And Ignorance the same.

But today he has a Rival
    As we roll down History's Track—
For the "Anti" on the Cartwheel
    Thinks she makes the Wheels go back!

To the Indifferent Women

A Sestina

You who are happy in a thousand homes,
Or overworked therein, to a dumb peace;
Whose souls are wholly centered in the life
Of that small group you personally love—
Who told you that you need not know or care
About the sin and sorrow of the world?

Do you believe the sorrow of the world
Does not concern you in your little homes?
That you are licensed to avoid the care
And toil for human progress, human peace,
And the enlargement of our power of love
Until it covers every field of life?

The one first duty of all human life
Is to promote the progress of the world
In righteousness, in wisdom, truth and love;
And you ignore it, hidden in your homes,
Content to keep them in uncertain peace,
Content to leave all else without your care.

Yet you are mothers! And a mother's care
Is the first step towards friendly human life,
Life where all nations in untroubled peace
Unite to raise the standard of the world
And make the happiness we seek in homes
Spread everywhere in strong and fruitful love.

You are content to keep that mighty love
In its first steps forever; the crude care
Of animals for mate and young and homes,
Instead of pouring it abroad in life,
Its mighty current feeding all the world
Till every human child shall grow in peace.

You cannot keep your small domestic peace,
Your little pool of undeveloped love,
While the neglected, starved, unmothered world
Struggles and fights for lack of mother's care,
And its tempestuous, bitter, broken life
Beats in upon you in your selfish homes.

We all may have our homes in joy and peace
When woman's life, in its rich power of love
Is joined with man's to care for all the world.

Women Do Not Want It

When the woman suffrage argument first stood upon its legs,
They answered it with cabbages, they answered it with eggs,
They answered it with ridicule, they answered it with scorn,
They thought it a monstrosity that should not have been born.

When the woman suffrage argument grew vigorous and wise,
And was not to be answered by these opposite replies,
They turned their opposition into reasoning severe
Upon the limitations of our God-appointed sphere.

We were told of disabilities—a long array of these,
Till one could think that womanhood was merely a disease;
And "the maternal sacrifice" was added to the plan
Of the various sacrifices we have always made—to man.

Religionists and scientists, in amity and bliss,
However else they disagreed, could all agree on this,
And the gist of all their discourse, when you got down in it,
Was—we could not have the ballot because we were not fit!

They would not hear the reason, they would not fairly yield,
They would not own their arguments were beaten in the field;
But time passed on, and someway, we need not ask them how,
Whatever ails those arguments—we do not hear them now!

You may talk of suffrage now with an educated man,
And he agrees with all you say, as sweetly as he can:
'T would be better for us all, of course, if womanhood was free;
But "the women do not want it"—and so it must not be!

'T is such a tender thoughtfulness! So exquisite a care!
Not to pile on our frail shoulders what we do not wish to bear!
But, oh, most generous brother! Let us look a little more—
Have we women always wanted what you gave to us before?

Did we ask for veils and harems in the Oriental races?
Did we beseech to be "unclean," shut out of sacred places?
Did we beg for scolding bridles and ducking stools to come?
And clamor for the beating stick no thicker than your thumb?

Did we ask to be forbidden from all the trades that pay?
Did we claim the lower wages for a man's full work today?
Have we petitioned for the laws wherein our shame is shown:
That not a woman's child—nor her own body—is her own?

What women want has never been a strongly acting cause,
When woman has been wronged by man in churches, customs, laws;
Why should he find this preference so largely in his way,
When he himself admits the right of what we ask today?

Song for Equal Suffrage

Day of hope and day of glory! After slavery and woe,
Comes the dawn of woman's freedom, and the light shall grow and
  grow
Until every man and woman equal liberty shall know,
        In Freedom marching on!

Woman's right is woman's duty! For our share in life we call!
Our will it is not weakened and our power it is not small.
We are half of every nation! We are mothers of them all!
        In Wisdom marching on!

Not for self but larger service has our cry for freedom grown,
There is crime, disease and warfare in a world of men alone,
In the name of love we're rising now to serve and save our own,
        As Peace comes marching on!

By every sweet and tender tie around our heartstrings curled,
In the cause of nobler motherhood is woman's flag unfurled,
Till every child shall know the joy and peace of mother's world—
        As Love comes marching on!

We will help to make a pruning hook of every outgrown sword,
We will help to knit the nations in continuing accord,
In humanity made perfect is the glory of the Lord,
        As His world goes marching on!

Another Star

(Suffrage Campaign Song for California)

Tune: "Buy a Broom."

There are five a-light before us,
In the flag flying o'er us,
There'll be six on next election—
        We bring a new star!
We are coming like the others,
Free Sisters, Free Brothers,
In the pride of our affection
        For California.
Chorus: A ballot for the Lady!
For the Home and for the Baby!
Come, vote ye for the Lady,
        The Baby, the Home!

Star of Hope and Star of Beauty!
Of Freedom! Of Duty!
Star of childhood's new protection,
        That rises so high!
We will work for it together
In the golden, gay weather,
And we'll have it next election,
        Or we will know why.
Chorus: A ballot for the Lady!
For the Home and for the Baby!
Come, vote ye for the Lady,
        The Baby, the Home!

She Who Is To Come

A woman—in so far as she beholdeth
    Her one Beloved's face;
A mother—with a great heart that enfoldeth
    The children of the Race;
A body, free and strong, with that high beauty
    That comes of perfect use, is built thereof;
A mind where Reason ruleth over Duty,
    And Justice reigns with Love;
A self-poised, royal soul, brave, wise and tender,
    No longer blind and dumb;
A Human Being, of an unknown splendor,
    Is she who is to come!

A Note About the Author

Charlotte Perkins Gilman (1860–1935) was an American author, feminist, and social reformer. Born in Hartford, Connecticut, Gilman was raised by her mother after her father abandoned his family to poverty. A single mother, Mary Perkins struggled to provide for her son and daughter, frequently enlisting the help of her estranged husband's aunts, including Harriet Beecher Stowe, the author of *Uncle Tom's Cabin*. These early experiences shaped Charlotte's outlook on gender and society, inspiring numerous written works and a lifetime of activism. Gilman excelled in school as a youth and went on to study at the Rhode Island School of Design where, in 1879, she met a woman named Martha Luther. The two were involved romantically for the next few years until Luther married in 1881. Distraught, Gilman eventually married Charles Walter Stetson, a painter, in 1884, with whom she had one daughter. After Katharine's birth, Gilman suffered an intense case of post-partum depression, an experience which inspired her landmark story "The Yellow Wallpaper" (1890). Gilman and Stetson divorced in 1894, after which Charlotte moved to California and became active in social reform. Gilman was a pioneer of the American feminist movement and an early advocate for women's suffrage, divorce, and euthanasia. Her radical beliefs and controversial views on race—Gilman was known to support white supremacist ideologies—nearly consigned her work to history; at the time of her death none of her works remained in print. In the 1970s, however, the rise of second-wave feminism and its influence on literary scholarship revived her reputation, bringing her work back into publication.

A Note from the Publisher

Spanning many genres, from non-fiction essays to literature classics to children's books and lyric poetry, Mint Edition books showcase the master works of our time in a modern new package. The text is freshly typeset, is clean and easy to read, and features a new note about the author in each volume. Many books also include exclusive new introductory material. Every book boasts a striking new cover, which makes it as appropriate for collecting as it is for gift giving. Mint Edition books are only printed when a reader orders them, so natural resources are not wasted. We're proud that our books are never manufactured in excess and exist only in the exact quantity they need to be read and enjoyed.

bookfinity™

Discover more of your favorite classics with Bookfinity™.

- Track your reading with custom book lists.
- Get great book recommendations for your personalized Reader Type.
- Add reviews for your favorite books.
- AND MUCH MORE!

Visit **bookfinity.com** and take the fun Reader Type quiz to get started.

Enjoy our classic and modern companion pairings!

Classic & Modern